Love to Dance

Ballroom

Angela Royston

Heinemann
LIBRARY
Chicago, Illinois

© 2013 Raintree
an imprint of Capstone Global Library, LLC
Chicago, Illinois

Edited by Nancy Dickmann, Catherine Veitch,
and Abby Colich
Designed by Cynthia Della-Rovere
Picture research by Elizabeth Alexander
Production by Alison Parsons
Originated by Capstone Global Library Ltd
Printed and bound in China by CTPS

16 15 14 13 12
10 9 8 7 6 5 4 3 2 1

Library of Congress Cataloging-in-Publication Data
Royston, Angela, 1945-
 Ballroom / Angela Royston.—1st ed.
  p. cm.—(Love to dance)
 Includes bibliographical references and index.
 ISBN 978-1-4109-4921-9 (hb)—ISBN 978-1-4109-
4926-4 (pb) 1. Ballroom dancing—Juvenile literature.
I. Title.
GV1751.R79 2013
793.3'3—dc23   2012019139

Acknowledgments
We would like to thank the following for permission to
reproduce photographs: Alamy pp. 6 (© North Wind
Picture Archives), 13 (© ZUMA Wire Service), 17 (©
Zbigniew Tomaszewski), 20 (© tarczas), 21 (© tarczas),
22 (© Jeff Gilbert), 23 (© Pictorial Press Ltd), 25 (©
Geoff A Howard), 26 (© RIA Novosti); Corbis pp. 7
(© Bettmann), 12 (© Michael Ochs Archives), 14 (©
yangzongyou/Xinhua Press), 24 (© Ilian Iliev/Lebrecht
Music & Arts), 28 (© Pittsburgh Post-Gazette/ZUMA
Press); Getty Images pp. 8 (DEA/A. DAGLI ORTI),
10 (Pailin Wedel/Raleigh News & Observer/MCT),
27 (Photo by 20th Century-Fox), 29 (Per-Anders
Pettersson); iStockphoto p. 18 (© Oleg Filipchuk);
Shutterstock pp. 5 (© akva), 9 (© Zzvet), 11 (© Igor
Bulgarin), 16 (© Anky); SuperStock title page (© Blend
Images), 4 (© Fancy Collection), 15 (© age footstock),
19 (© Prisma).

Design features reproduced with permission of
Shutterstock (© Nejron Photo, © Roman Sigaev).

Front cover photograph of ballroom dancers reproduced
with permission of Shutterstock (© Zzvet).

We would like to thank Allen Desterhaft for his
invaluable help in the preparation of this book.

Contents

Some words are shown in bold, **like this**. You can find out what they mean by looking in the glossary.

This Is Ballroom Dancing!

Two dancers glide together across the floor. She is wearing high heels and a glamorous dress. Their feet move in perfect time to the music. They are taking part in a competition for ballroom dancers, called **DanceSport**.

What is it all about?

Cheryl Burke, a ballroom dance teacher, says, "Ballroom to me was so exciting—the music, the costumes…"

Where Ballroom Began

Ballroom dancing began in royal palaces and the large houses of rich people. That is why dancers today still wear **formal** suits and fancy ball gowns.

The minuet

The minuet was popular just before 1800. The dancers followed set moves and steps. They made graceful patterns as they moved across the dance floor.

Waltzing

After 1800, people began to dance a new dance, the Viennese **waltz**. Each couple danced close together and stayed together for the whole dance. Today, two waltzes are danced—the Viennese and the slow waltz.

This painting shows couples dancing the Viennese waltz.

How shocking!

In the 1800s, many people disapproved of waltzing. They thought it was wrong for a man and woman to dance so close together!

Take Your Partners...

In ballroom dancing, a man and a woman dance together as partners. **DanceSport** partners spend many hours practicing their dance moves. They want to dance perfectly in the next competition!

The closed hold

Each dance usually begins with the dance partners standing in the closed hold. This hold helps them to keep time together.

The Jazz Age

In the early 1900s, ballroom dancers began dancing to **jazz**. This exciting style of music was invented by African Americans. It led to many different dances, including the **Lindy Hop**.

The Lindy Hop

The most famous Lindy Hopper was Frankie Manning. He introduced spectacular moves, such as flipping his partner over his head!

Dance Style: The Quickstep

The **quickstep** is a popular ballroom dance. The dancers move quickly and easily around the floor. The dance is made up of a slow step followed by two quick steps, and then another slow step.

Hops and twirls

The two quick steps allow the dancers to twirl, hop, skip, and spin. They look as if they are flying!

What to Wear

Women and girls' dresses are often covered with sequins, feathers, or sparkling rhinestones, which look like diamonds. Women wear high-heeled shoes.

Dressed to impress!

Men often wear suits and leather shoes. The suit can be **formal**, such as a **tail suit**, or it can be specially designed for the dance.

17

Dance Style: The Tango

The **tango** is one of the best-known dances. The dancers stand upright and then walk together forward, backward, or to the side. This is called the promenade.

Eye-catching

The dancers may pause between one sequence of steps and the next. During the pause, the woman poses in a **dramatic**, eye-catching position.

Competitive Ballroom

In competitions, ballroom dances are divided into standard ballroom and Latin ballroom. The standard ballroom dances are the **quickstep**, the foxtrot, the slow **waltz**, the **tango**, and the Viennese waltz.

Latin ballroom

The Latin dances are the cha cha cha, samba, rumba, paso doble, and the jive. In Latin ballroom, the dancers often dance farther apart.

Dance Style: The Jive

The jive includes twists and turns, with the dancers changing position. In **DanceSport**, the basic step is two rocking steps and then three small steps to each side.

KERRY MILLS CAKE WALK

MR. MILLS
IS THE ORIGINATOR
OF THE CAKE WALK.

YOU UNDOUBTEDLY
RECALL HIS FAMOUS
COMPOSITIONS :
"THE GEORGIA CAMPMEETING,"
"WHISTLING RUFUS"
"RASTUS ON PARADE"

F.A. MILLS

The cake walk

Jive competitions began around the 1880s. The dance was called the cake walk, because the prize was a cake.

And the Winner Is ...

Today, few young people dance ballroom dances, except in competitions. **DanceSport** is popular in many countries. In wheelchair DanceSport, one of the partners uses a wheelchair.

Biggest competition

The biggest international competition is held in Blackpool, England. Dancers from about 50 countries take part.

Where to See Ballroom Dancing

You do not have to go far to see ballroom dancing. There are several dance shows on television. In some, a professional dancer works with a celebrity.

Dance shows are seen on television around the world. This version of *Dancing with the Stars* was shown on Russian television.

Dance movies

Several movies are about ballroom dancing. In the 1940s and 1950s, Fred Astaire was a big star. Above, he dances with Leslie Caron in *Daddy Long Legs*.

Give It a Try!

Ballroom is fun to watch, but it is even better to dance. Look for classes for children in your neighborhood. You just need comfortable clothes—no high heels!

A new you

Ballroom dancing is a good way to exercise and make friends. Dancing will help you feel more confident about yourself.

Glossary

DanceSport ballroom dancing performed in a competition, rather than just for fun

dramatic describes something that stands out and catches your attention

formal dressy, according to a set of rules

jazz type of music that has strong rhythm and allows musicians to play the music the way they like

Lindy Hop style of dance that began in New York City. It was danced to jazz music.

quickstep standard ballroom dance in which the dancers spin, run, and jump around the dance floor

tail suit suit with a formal jacket that is short in the front but has two long "tails" in the back

tango romantic standard ballroom dance that began in Argentina

waltz first standard ballroom dance. It has two forms: the Viennese waltz, which came from Austria in the 1800s, and the slow waltz, which began in the 1920s.

Find Out More

Books

Blizin Gillis, Jennifer. *Ballroom Dancing for Fun*!
Minneapolis, Minn.: Compass Point, 2008.

Freese, Joan. *Ballroom Dancing* (Snap Books).
Mankato, Minn.: Capstone, 2008.

Hamilton, Sue. *Ballroom* (Xtreme Dance).
Edina, Minn.: ABDO, 2011.

Underwood, Deborah. *Ballroom Dancing* (Culture in
Action). Chicago: Raintree, 2010.

Websites

Facthound offers a safe, fun way to find Internet sites related
to this book. All of the sites on Facthound have been
researched by our staff.

Here's all you do:
Visit www.facthound.com

Type in this code: 9781410949219

Index